POLITICS TODAY

WHO ARE CONSERVATIVES and What Do They Believe In?

Cathleen Small

Cavendish Square
New York

Published in 2020 by Cavendish Square Publishing, LLC
243 5th Avenue, Suite 136, New York, NY 10016

First Edition

Library of Congress Cataloging-in-Publication Data

Names: Small, Cathleen, author.
Title: Who are conservatives and what do they believe in? / Cathleen D. Small.
Description: First edition. | New York : Cavendish Square, 2020. | Series: Politics today | Includes bibliographical references and index. | Audience: Grades 7-12.
Identifiers: LCCN 2018049866 (print) | LCCN 2019002148 (ebook) | ISBN 9781502645142 (ebook) | ISBN 9781502645135 (library bound) | ISBN 9781502645128 (pbk.)
Subjects: LCSH: Conservatism--United States--Juvenile literature.
Classification: LCC JC573.2.U6 (ebook) | LCC JC573.2.U6 S62 2020 (print) | DDC 320.520973--dc23
LC record available at https://lccn.loc.gov/2018049866

Editorial Director: David McNamara
Editor: Lauren Wehner
Copy Editor: Nathan Heidelberger
Associate Art Director: Alan Sliwinski
Designer: Jessica Nevins
Production Coordinator: Karol Szymczuk
Photo Research: J8 Media

The photographs in this book are used by permission and through the courtesy of: Cover (left column- top to bottom) AXL/Shutterstock.com, Lane V. Erickson/Shutterstock.com, 3dfoto/Shutterstock.com, (right) M Dogan/Shutterstock.com; p. 4 Chip Somodevilla/Getty Images; p. 6 Christophel Fine Art/UIG/Getty Images; p. 9 Pew Research Center; p. 10 (left, right) Duane Prokop/Getty Images for MoveOn.org, Sergio Flores/Bloomberg via Getty Images; p. 11 Nicholas Kamm/AFP/Getty Images; p. 13 Ron Sachs-Pool/Getty Images; p. 14 JPL Designs/Shutterstock.com; p. 16 Xinhua/Alamy Stock Photo; p. 17 Luke Sharrett/Bloomberg/Getty Images; p. 18 FatCamera/E+/Getty Images; p. 21 Gal Roma/AFP/Newscom; p. 22, 31 Mark Reinstein/Shutterstock.com; p. 23 Olivier Douliery/Getty Images; p. 26 David Ryder/Bloomberg/Getty Images; p. 28 Roy Scott/ikon Images/Getty Images; p. 30 Ralph Eleaser Whiteside Earl/Wikimedia Commons/File:Andrew jackson head.jpg/Public Domain; p. 34 Fotosearch/Getty Images; p. 37 Mario Tama/Getty Images; p. 40 Bettmann/Getty Images; p. 43 Crush Rush/Shutterstock.com; p. 44 Dirck Halstead/Time & Life Pictures/Getty Images; p. 46 Senate Television/AP Images; p. 48 Tim Sloan/AFP/Getty Images; p. 50 Ron Sachs/Bloomberg/Getty Images.

Printed in the United States of America

★ Contents

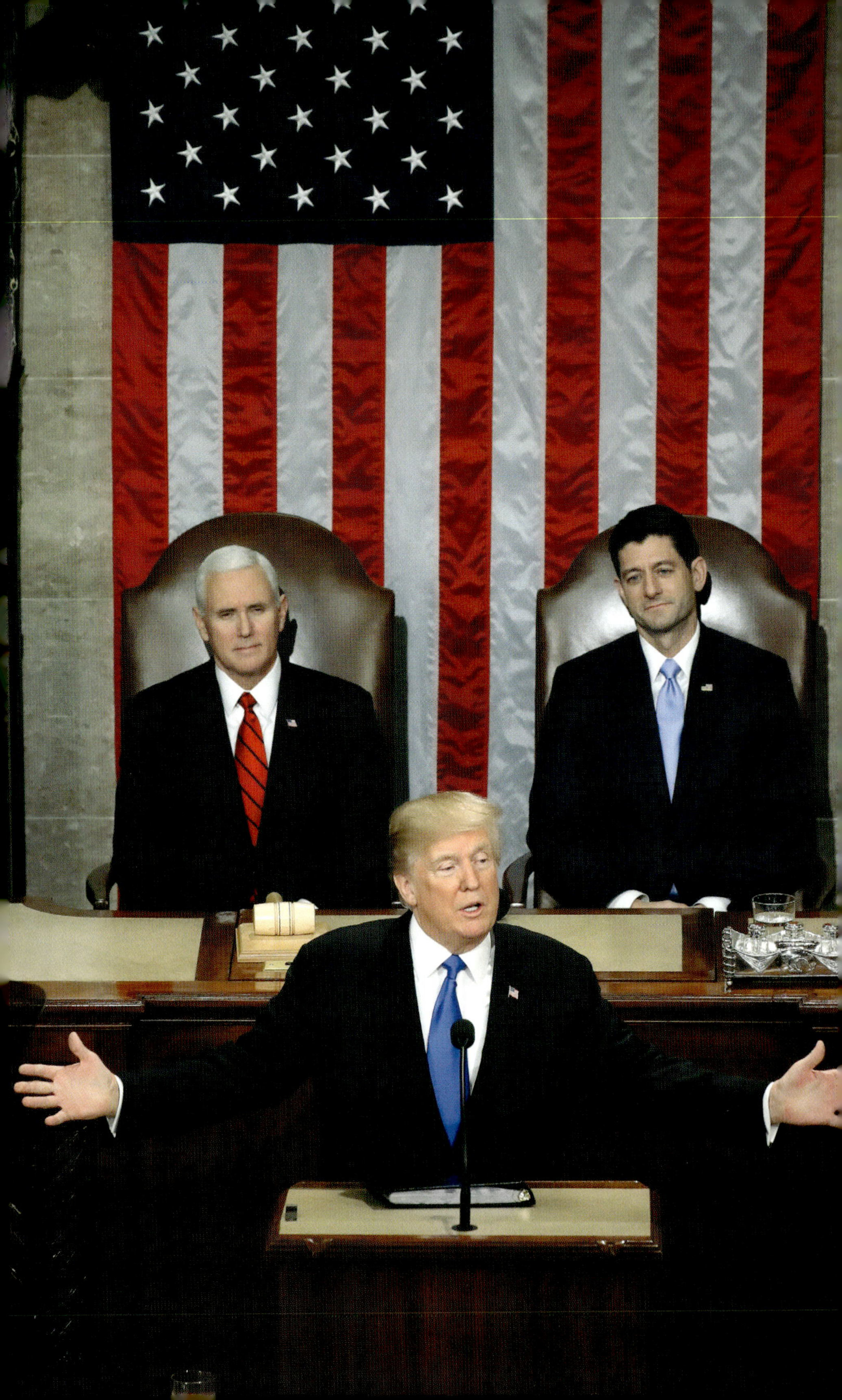

★ Chapter 1

What Makes a Conservative

The political climate in the United States has been heated for a number of years, and it does not seem likely to cool down anytime soon. With the rise of social media, where some people feel comfortable engaging in angry rants against those with differing political views and opinions, and where there are questions about the validity of news and information, the divide between conservatives and liberals seems to be growing. To be able to understand the conservative viewpoint—and that of many people who consider themselves part of the Republican political party—one must first understand who conservatives are and what they believe in.

Generally, people use the terms "Republican" and "conservative" interchangeably, and they do the same with the words "liberal" and "Democrat." However, to do so is incorrect. In reality, "Republican" and "Democrat" are terms used to describe members of two prominent political parties in the United States, and "conservative" and "liberal" are terms

Opposite: In 2018, President Donald Trump delivered the State of the Union Address as Vice President Mike Pence (*rear left*) and Speaker of the House Paul Ryan (*rear right*) looked on. All three men are conservative members of the Republican Party.

used to describe people who subscribe to certain political, philosophical, and social ideologies.

A History of Conservatism

While conservative ideals have existed as long as humans have lived in civilized societies with widely accepted norms, conservatism in a political context is relatively new. Conservatism in politics is thought to have originated in the late eighteenth and early nineteenth centuries, around the time the French Revolution and the American Revolution broke out.

How conservatism manifested was a little different in each conflict given their distinct contexts and the unique factors leading to each conflict. Generally, however, conservatism favored holding on to tradition. Conservatives did not support change and wanted to see their respective societies continue to uphold the traditions that had long been in place. Therefore, they were more likely to oppose both revolutions: in the case of the United States, because they wanted

This oil painting depicts the storming of the Bastille in Paris on July 14, 1789, during the French Revolution.

England to maintain its sovereignty over the colonies; and in the case of the French Revolution, because they supported the monarchy.

Early conservatism also supported a free market and a capitalist society where the powerful could retain their power and wealth, and the less powerful could attempt to work their way toward more power. This is in sharp contrast to socialist and communist ideologies, which favor societies where wealth and power are distributed equally and are regulated by the community, and where property is publicly owned. In other words, socialists and communists favor "sharing the wealth," whereas conservatives have historically favored a society that allowed people to be the makers of their own fortune.

As is normally the case, there are pros and cons to all of these ideologies. For example, distributing wealth equally may be a great idea in theory, but when there is not enough wealth to go around, it can result in widespread poverty and even famine. On the other hand, in a capitalist society, people can work their way to the top—but for those who begin with more obstacles to surmount than others, it can be an incredibly limiting system in which they are forever struggling to get by.

No ideology, however, can be described in entirely black-and-white terms. Conservatives may believe in some elements of socialism, whereas liberals may believe in some elements of a capitalist society. For example, in the 2016 presidential election, US senator Bernie Sanders was a relatively popular candidate—even among some conservatives—despite generally favoring a socialist economy. The winner of the 2016 election, President Donald Trump, favors many capitalist ideals (he is a businessman by trade), yet he has not always supported free trade or reduced government spending.

US Conservatives by Political Party

It is difficult to determine the exact demographics of conservatives because it's a self-applied label. Democrats and Republicans can be tracked by looking at voter-registration records, but citizens don't register as conservatives. They are often (but not always) Republicans, but a fair number of Democrats also consider themselves conservative.

According to Gallup, a well-known polling and analytics agency, 35 percent of adults in the United States considered themselves conservative as of 2018. That's compared to 26 percent who considered themselves liberal. Another 35 percent of people identified themselves as "moderate"—that is, somewhere between the two ideologies.

What ideology a person identifies with doesn't necessarily correspond to the political party he or she supports. Although the Democratic Party is popularly associated with liberalism, in 2001, 25 percent of Democrats actually considered themselves conservative (with 30 percent considering themselves liberal and 44 percent considering themselves moderate). However, that has begun to change: as of 2017, only 13 percent considered themselves conservative, while 50 percent said they were liberal. The remaining 35 percent who responded to the poll considered themselves moderate.

The same trend toward liberalism is not present among Republicans. According to Gallup's polls, 62 percent of Republicans considered themselves conservative in 2001, and only 6 percent considered themselves liberal. (The remaining 31 percent who answered considered themselves moderate.) By 2017, these numbers had not changed very much: 69 percent of Republicans considered themselves conservative, while only 5 percent considered themselves liberal. Meanwhile, 25 percent considered themselves moderate.

Overall, there has been an ideological shift toward liberalism among Democrats over the past two decades, but there has not been much of a shift in ideology among Republicans. The Republican Party is still heavily conservative, and the Democratic Party is still relatively balanced, but with a trend toward liberal ideology in recent years. The result, some believe, has been increasing polarization between the two parties—that is, there now seems to be a wider ideological gap between the two than there was two decades ago.

Sharp differences in partisan, ideological identifications between younger and older generations

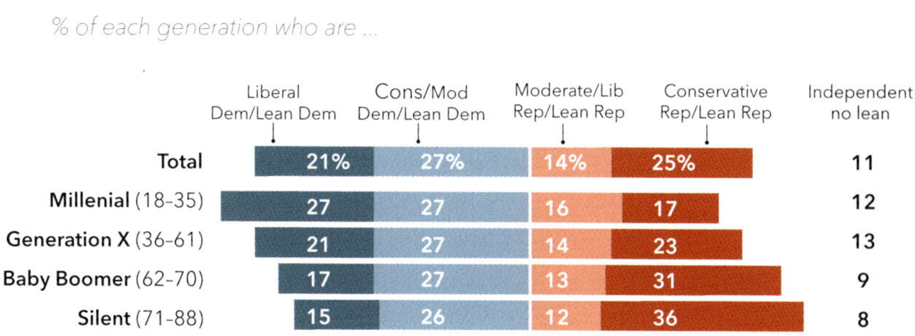

Note: "Don't know" responses not shown.
Source: Based on merged Pew Research Center surveys conducted in 2016.

PEW RESEARCH CENTER

In 2016, the Pew Research Center tracked liberal vs. moderate vs. conservative ideology based on age group. This is what Pew learned.

During the 2016 presidential election, Bernie Sanders (*left*) received some support from conservatives, despite promoting liberal policies. Meanwhile, Donald Trump (*right*) supported some liberal economic policies, despite being seen largely as conservative.

In other words, most people straddle the line between conservative and liberal, capitalism and socialism. There are people who are extremely conservative, or "right-wing," and people who are extremely left-wing, but they are not the norm.

Conservatism in the United States

Those who fall right of center in their ideology are usually considered conservatives. In the United States, conservatives are generally highly patriotic and support American traditions. This is paired with widespread support of reduced government spending, and opposition to "big government"—that is, government that interferes too much in citizens' rights.

Some American conservatives—though certainly not all—believe that their ideology is linked with Christian values. For example, on social media and in various news outlets, some people talk about the "war on Christmas." This phrase is drawn from conservative values: conservatives generally believe that, because the Founding Fathers of the United States were Christian, Christmas (a Christian holiday) should be celebrated as a nationally recognized holiday. Liberals, on the other hand, believe that, because the United States is a melting pot of cultures, it is more inclusive to refer to "the holiday season" in more general terms, so that it can include such holidays as Christmas, Hanukkah, Kwanzaa, and Diwali—all of which fall in the autumn and winter.

Former president Barack Obama is a Christian who believes that holidays of other faiths should be recognized as well.

As is often the case, this disagreement can get blown out of proportion, and generate nationwide controversies. However, in the end, liberals are not trying to bring about the downfall of Christmas, and conservatives are not trying to prevent Jewish people from celebrating Hanukkah, African Americans from celebrating Kwanzaa, or Hindus from celebrating Diwali. This supposed "war on Christmas" is mostly the result of inflammatory rhetoric.

In the United States, conservatives also generally support a capitalist free market, where supply and demand are driven by consumers and competition, rather than by government regulation. In fact, conservatives in the United States typically favor minimal government intervention in business, economics, and some social matters. When liberals are in political power, more laws are often passed that regulate business entities, and when conservatives are in power, it is not uncommon for the government to repeal, or cancel, the legislation passed by liberals. In his first year in office, for example, President Trump repealed a number of regulations on businesses and education. It was not an unusual move for a conservative politician to make.

Instead of government intervention and regulations, conservatives typically believe that many decisions regarding finances and the economy should be made by people and their families. This can be appealing to those who want the freedom to run a business in the way they want to, without having to conform to the regulations set by the government. On paper, that sounds appealing to most people. However, this ideology does not usually favor labor unions and the collective power they bring. For people who are not running a business–for members of the working class, for example–this can be a major negative. The people employed at lower levels of a company often rely on labor unions to ensure that they are paid a fair wage and have appropriate working conditions.

Not all conservatives oppose labor unions, and business owners who do oppose labor unions do not necessarily provide poor wages and working conditions. However, the opposition to regulation is one part of the conservative ideology that doesn't necessarily appeal to some people. For example, if they are in the working class and are not business owners, they may feel uncomfortable in a working situation that is not regulated or does not have union involvement.

Conservatives also typically oppose high taxes. Taxes are often used to fund social programs that help people in need, and so higher taxes often mean more money is available to help those in need. Liberals favor social programs, such as food stamps and Medicaid, that provide assistance to people who need financial help. Conservatives, however, typically do not believe that the money collected from high taxes really does much to help people in need. They sometimes cite cases of people who "work the system" and live off government aid, even though many may actually be capable of working for their own living. For example, conservative politician Paul Ryan, the Speaker of the House of Representatives at the beginning of Donald Trump's presidency, spoke often of his desire to dismantle Medicaid, whereas Senator Kamala Harris, a liberal from California, is a staunch supporter of social programs.

Former representative Paul Ryan was an advocate for dismantling Medicaid.

It is highly unlikely that politicians such as Ryan want to see harm come to the people who may suffer if Medicaid is dismantled; rather, they hold the conservative view that the federal government should not be responsible for handling a social program like Medicaid. They add that, in many cases, they don't believe such progams actually work for the people who rely on them. It's easy for those who support social programs to be frustrated with what seems like a disregard for people who are struggling, but in reality, this disagreement often just comes down to a difference in ideology: conservatives believe that the federal government should have a minimal role in social programs.

LEGISLATIVE

EXECUTIVE

JUDICIAL

★ Chapter 2

Politics and Government

People who identify as conservative can come from any political party, so it is important to first understand the core beliefs that conservative people hold. More important than knowing whether conservatives identify as Republican, Democrat, or independent is understanding the values and beliefs they hold that inform their voting decisions in elections.

Big Versus Small Government

The government plays a large role in the lives of people living in the United States. It establishes and upholds the laws that citizens live by, and it funds key financial, economic, infrastructural, and social programs. The government also controls the flow of citizens coming into the United States. It is fair to say that, in some ways, the government affects the life of every person, every day.

There are two main ideologies about the role of government: first, that the government should regulate many

Opposite: The US government is made up of the legislative, executive, and judicial branches.

In a joint session of Congress, members from both the Senate and the House of Representatives are present.

issues affecting US citizens; and the opposing view, that the government should have a minimal role in people's lives.

Liberals believe in more government involvement. They generally tend to favor government regulations that may help drive the country in the direction they want to see it go. For example, liberals favor environmental regulations that will help slow the harmful effects of climate change and pollution. Liberals also favor educational regulations that are put in place to try to ensure that all children in the United States can receive a high-quality education.

These are admirable goals: Who doesn't want to see children get a good education? Who doesn't want to see the environment preserved? Inflammatory rhetoric in the press would have people believe that, because conservatives don't usually support government regulations and involvement, they don't care about things like the environment and education.

One must cut through the rhetoric to understand the conservative viewpoint. Regulations are expensive to uphold, and in the view of conservatives, they often do not accomplish what they set out to do. Conservatives, therefore, believe that the federal government should not get involved in these matters, and should instead leave citizens and state governments to sort them out. They believe that individual citizens should be empowered to solve their own problems, and only when they cannot should the state should step in.

Conservatives also tend to be fiscally conservative. This means, among other things, that they believe the increased taxes and government debt needed to enforce government regulations and fund government programs are not a wise use of money. They prefer to keep taxes lower and reduce debt, which can be accomplished, in part, by removing regulations and leaving individual citizens and states to handle many issues that liberals feel should be handled by the federal government.

Bulldozers move coal at a West Virginia plant in 2015. The coal industry has experienced widespread job loss in recent decades. Some conservatives favor cutting environmental regulations, which they believe will bring coal jobs back.

In the eyes of conservatives, the US economy functions best when the federal government is kept small and its influence is kept to a minimum.

Individual Rights

The conservative view that government should be kept small means that individual citizens are held more accountable. It is up to them to solve their own problems–or sometimes, it is up to the state government.

For example, there are education regulations on both the federal and state levels. It is not left only to the federal government to put such rules in place. In 2009, the "Common Core" education initiative was set forth by the National Governors Association; it has impacted and set curriculum standards in most states nationwide. The state of New York, on the other hand, has further requirements, called Regents, which must be passed to graduate from high school. The Board of Regents of the State of New York started

The Individuals with Disabilities Education Act was put in place to ensure that children with disabilities have full access to public education.

administering these exams in 1865, and they have adapted to changes in curriculum as time has passed.

An example of a presidential administration taking direct action in the realm of education is the Individuals with Disabilities Education Act (IDEA), which was first signed into law under a different name by President Gerald Ford in 1975. Protections for those with disabilities were expanded under Republican president George H. W. Bush. This was not a very conservative move by President Bush, since IDEA essentially puts the federal government in charge of ensuring that students with disabilities receive what is known as a "free and appropriate public education." Typically, conservatives believe issues like this are best handled at the state level.

Under the Trump administration, which is largely conservative, the president and his cabinet have attempted to remove federal IDEA regulatory guidance, indicating that they prefer that states handle education issues with regard to students with disabilities.

The liberal response to these efforts has been largely negative, because handing control of disability education rights over to fifty individual states means that students with disabilities might have certain rights in one state but not in another. Given that just a few decades ago many students with disabilities were banned from even attending public schools, many in the disability community feel it is critically important that the federal government remain involved and ensure that across the nation students with disabilities will retain their right to be educated.

Conversely, there are other individual rights issues in which conservatives believe the government should play a bigger part. Two examples are in the areas of reproductive rights and marriage rights. Conservatives believe the

The Power of the Judicial Branch

The United States government has three parts, known as branches: the executive branch, which consists of the president and cabinet; the legislative branch, which consists of the Senate and the House of Representatives; and the judicial branch, which includes the Supreme Court. All branches perform different functions and are equally important, but the Supreme Court is particularly influential in making decisions about what types of laws are permissible in the United States.

The Supreme Court is in charge of upholding the Constitution and handing down legal decisions that can set precedent for decisions in lower courts and can change state laws. Thus, the ideology of the court plays a large part in shaping the legal landscape of the United States.

For a long time, the court was relatively balanced in the ideologies represented—it had some liberal judges, some conservative, and some moderate. However, the extremely conservative justice Antonin Scalia died in early 2016, leaving a seat open on the bench.

Supreme Court justices are appointed by the president and confirmed by the Senate. They are appointed for life terms. When Justice Scalia died, Democrat Barack Obama was the president. He attempted to appoint Merrick Garland, who was generally considered to be a moderate liberal, to the open seat. At that time, however, the Senate was controlled by Republicans and was largely conservative, so they refused to confirm Garland's appointment. Naturally, the conservative Senate wanted Justice Scalia's conservative seat filled by another conservative.

When President Trump took office, conservatives in the government hoped he would appoint a conservative justice to fill Justice Scalia's seat. In 2017, President Trump nominated Neil Gorsuch, a conservative judge who was confirmed by the Senate.

In 2018, Justice Anthony Kennedy, a moderate conservative, retired, leaving yet another seat on the bench open. President Trump nominated Brett Kavanaugh, who was known to have an extremely conservative voting record, to fill the seat. Kavanaugh was confirmed in October 2018, causing the court to swing to the conservative side, with five conservative or moderately conservative justices, compared to four liberal justices.

As of 2018, Justice Ruth Bader Ginsburg, a liberal, was the oldest serving justice on the court. Many liberals hoped she would choose to step down while Barack Obama was still president, so that he could appoint another liberal to fill her seat. However, some questioned whether President Obama could get a liberal justice approved by the conservative Senate. If Justice Ginsburg or any other liberal justice on the bench were to end his or her term during a Republican administration, the balance of the Supreme Court could tip even farther to the right, which some liberals fear would result in decisions such as *Roe v. Wade* being overturned.

The justices of the US Supreme Court are pictured in late 2018.

government should step in where these issues are concerned, citing family values, the Bible, and tradition.

Reproductive rights and marriage rights are addressed as part of an ideology known as social conservatism. Conservatives believe that the people of the United States should hold on to historical traditions and beliefs, which in some cases are influenced by religion. Although many of the original colonists who came to America were looking for religious freedom, once they were established, the new settlements and colonies were often driven in their systems of governance by religious beliefs.

In the colonial era of the United States, most of the settlers who arrived in America were Christian. Today, the United States is a melting pot of people who practice different religions, but it is still heavily Christian. Conservatives generally think that those early traditions and beliefs, often informed by Christianity, should be upheld.

In Washington, DC, in 1989, pro-life and pro-choice advocates face off in demonstrations outside the US Supreme Court building.

Conservative opinions around reproductive rights are informed by such beliefs. Christianity teaches that life begins at the moment a baby is conceived, and certain branches of Christianity, such as Catholicism, consider it a sin to have an abortion or use birth control. In fact, depending on the branch of Christianity, abortion and birth control are sometimes considered to be murder–ethically, if not in the eyes of the law.

Social conservatives believe that abortion should be illegal on a national level (though many consider birth control acceptable). While those in favor of legalized abortion argue that a woman has a right to choose, social conservatives who oppose abortion argue that the unborn fetus has a right to be born. They feel that terminating a pregnancy is a violation of the unborn fetus's human rights.

Similarly, religion has informed conservative views on marriage. Social conservatives believe that marriage

Advocates for and against gay rights demonstrate outside the US Supreme Court in 2015 as the court considers whether same-sex marriage should be legal.

is defined in the Bible—a collection of sacred Jewish and Christian texts—as being between one man and one woman. They argue that marriage should therefore only be legal between heterosexual couples—one male and one female, as defined by their sex at birth. This is in contrast to liberals, who are in favor of marriage equality. Liberals argue that a religious text should not be used to inform law and that marriage should be between two consenting adults, regardless of sex or gender. Liberals also often point out that the United States Constitution does not mention marriage, and thus marriage should not be regulated by the government.

Liberals fear that a socially conservative Supreme Court could mean the overturning of *Roe v. Wade*, the case law legalizing abortion. They also fear that marriage equality could be threatened if *Obergefell v. Hodges*, the landmark 2015 ruling that required all fifty states to perform and recognize marriages between same-sex couples, were overturned.

Another hot-button issue for conservatives and liberals is the right to bear arms, or gun rights. Generally, liberals favor stricter gun-control laws, whereas social conservatives defend the constitutional right of citizens to own firearms. This disagreement highlights the differences in how the Constitution is viewed by followers of the two ideologies.

Interpretation of the Constitution

The Constitution is the supreme law of the land in the United States. When a court case cannot be decided on the basis of state or local laws, it can be appealed to the US Supreme Court. If the case brings up the issue of whether something is a violation of constitutional law, then the court may choose to hear the case. The justices on the Supreme Court then hear arguments from all sides and deliver a ruling.

For example, when marriage equality was being debated, the case went all the way to the Supreme Court because part of the debate concerned whether allowing states *not* to recognize same-sex marriage was a violation of the Fourteenth Amendment to the Constitution—specifically, was it a violation of the due process and equal protection clauses of that amendment?

Supreme Court justices must constantly interpret the Constitution when hearing and deciding cases. There are multiple ways they can do so. One major method of interpreting the Constitution is viewing it as a "living document." People who view the Constitution as a living document believe that the original words of the Constitution need to be interpreted on the basis of current beliefs and societal norms. Liberal justices such as Ruth Bader Ginsburg typically favor a living-document interpretation.

Conservatives often read the Constitution from an originalist standpoint. Some originalists believe that the Constitution should be interpreted as the men who drafted and ratified it intended it to be interpreted. However, more originalists believe that the Constitution should be interpreted in the way that ordinary, everyday people in the 1780s would have understood it.

Originalists also believe that the amendments to the Constitution should be legally applied based on when they were written. That is to say, the amendments in the Bill of Rights should be applied either based on what the men who wrote them intended or, more likely, what citizens in 1791 would have understood them to mean.

Gun-rights advocates demonstrate outside the Washington State capitol building in 2018 in response to a wave of anti-gun protests after a school shooting in Florida.

While there are always exceptions to any rule, conservatives tend to be originalists, while liberals are more likely to look at the Constitution as a living document. This divide between the two approaches may be most evident when it comes to the Second Amendment to the Constitution: the right to bear arms.

The Second Amendment states, "A well regulated militia, being necessary to the security of a free state, the right of the people to keep and bear arms, shall not be infringed." In other words, people have the right to own weapons.

Many conservatives interpret the amendment literally—that citizens should be allowed to own weapons, period. As originalists, they argue that this is how the amendment would have been understood when it was written. However, many liberals argue that when the text of the Second Amendment was written, weapons were relatively simple firearms that required people to fire once, then stop and reload. Today's firearms include semiautomatic and automatic weapons, and there are high-capacity magazines that enable a person to fire large amounts of ammunition before stopping and reloading. Liberals argue that, had the Founding Fathers realized that guns would become so deadly, they probably would have wanted to limit widespread access to such weapons. This is an example of a living-document approach to the amendment.

Many liberals feel that the number of mass shootings in the United States would decrease greatly if high-capacity magazines and semiautomatic and automatic weapons were heavily restricted, and if there were more stringent background checks on people buying guns. Conservatives who are in favor of gun ownership typically believe that current background checks are sufficient and that citizens should be responsible for their own actions where weapons are concerned. They often argue that guns don't kill people—people kill people. Thus, they insist, there is no reason to penalize law-abiding citizens by restricting their right to bear arms.

Just as some legislators are conservative and some are liberal (and some are moderate), the same is true with the general population. Some citizens firmly support the Second Amendment and their right to bear arms, and others feel stronger safeguards should be in place with regard to weapons.

★ Chapter 3

Conservatism and the Economy

Conservatism takes many forms, including religious conservatism, social conservatism, and fiscal conservatism. When it comes to what is best for the nation's economy, fiscal conservatives have specific ideas on government spending, taxation, deregulation, privatization, and free trade.

Conservatives on Government Spending

The United States has almost always been in debt—massive debt, by personal standards. In 2018, for example, the national debt was roughly $21 trillion. In the history of the United States, there was only one brief period, under President Andrew Jackson, when the nation was not in debt. Typically, the debt grows every year.

Conservatives are opposed to increasing the national debt. Instead, the conservative philosophy on government spending is that the government should try to run under a balanced budget rather than increasing debt. Having a

Opposite: The national debt is a moving target: it varies from year to year. Conservatives and liberals have a difference of opinion when it comes to how the debt should be lowered, with conservatives arguing for lower government spending.

Andrew Jackson is the only president to ever lead the country during a period when there was zero national debt.

balanced budget means the government doesn't spend more money than it takes in.

Many liberals feel that if there is a need for government spending, that need can be covered by increasing taxes. However, fiscal conservatives prefer to keep taxes lower, and so if spending *must* be done in one area, they will advocate for reducing spending in other areas, rather than raising taxes. Indeed, fiscal conservatives may be inclined to view some spending as unnecessary and simply a means to increase the size of government.

Conservatives on Taxes

When George H. W. Bush ran for president in 1988 as a conservative representing the Republican Party, he famously said at the Republican National Convention, "Read my lips: no new taxes!" His economic plan for the United States largely followed that of fellow conservative Republican Ronald Reagan, who served as president of the United States from 1981 to 1989. Both fiscal conservatives felt that the way to spur the economy was to either keep taxes stable or to reduce them, rather than raising them.

This economic plan is part of what is known as supply-side economics, and it has been favored by a number of fiscal conservatives. The theory of supply-side economics is that decreasing taxes and government regulations will

In his campaign for the presidency, George H. W. Bush appealed to fiscal conservatives by declaring: "No new taxes!" Bush was elected president in 1988.

help stimulate the economy. Citizens will have more money in their pockets to spend, thanks to lowered taxes, and businesses will be able to operate more efficiently with fewer regulations in place.

While not everyone found Reagan's economic policies to be successful, many fiscal conservatives do cite them as effective. George H. W. Bush initially criticized Reagan's plans, but he later went along with them. Unfortunately for Bush, he was unable to fulfill his campaign promise of "no new taxes," and some say that's the reason he did not win a second term as president.

There are many different economic propositions for keeping the United States economy in check, but in general, the plans that fiscal conservatives embrace are the ones that involve keeping taxes low. Higher taxes, they argue, result in less spending by individual citizens and businesses, which can lead to economic recession and depression.

The Many Types of Conservatism

Conservatism can manifest in a variety of ways, but people are often a blend of conservative and liberal. For example, there is a group of Democrats in Congress, commonly known as the Blue Dog Coalition, who consider themselves to be conservative Democrats. Many people consider former president Bill Clinton to be a conservative Democrat.

Liberals are considered the left wing of the political spectrum, and conservatives are considered the right wing. Those who fall between the two are known as "moderates."

"Liberal conservatives" are usually fiscally conservative but also support a strong state government and social programs.

"Libertarian conservatives" are fiscally conservative and also heavily focus on individual liberties. They fall to the right on the political spectrum.

"Cultural conservatives" embrace traditional values and the preservation of what is perceived as a nation's common heritage.

"Social conservatives" embrace established social customs and traditional values. They tend not to favor large-scale social change, such as the national shift from marriage being between a man and a woman to marriage equality for same-sex couples.

"Religious conservatives" believe that religious teachings should inform politics and law.

"Progressive conservatives" tend toward the left side of the conservative political spectrum. They generally support social programs designed to help citizens in need, even while embracing other generally conservative beliefs.

"Authoritarian conservatives" are far on the right wing of the political spectrum, with strong support of religious and national institutions and traditions.

Recession, Depression, and the Economy

The United States has undergone several recessions or depressions in the last century. The most significant was the Great Depression of the 1930s, which was kicked off when the stock market crashed on Black Tuesday: October 29, 1929. The Great Depression was a worldwide event. It was caused by a combination of factors, including the fall of the stock market, a severe drought that greatly impacted the United States' agricultural industry, increasing unemployment rates, and decreased spending by citizens. No one factor can be blamed for a complete collapse of the economy.

When the Great Depression hit, conservatives were in power in the government. Republican Herbert Hoover took office as president in early 1929, just months before the stock market crash. He used many strategies to try to stimulate the economy, including a decidedly non-conservative move to increase taxes in an attempt to balance the government budget.

Frustrated Americans voted Democrat Franklin D. Roosevelt (FDR) into office after Hoover's one presidential term. Collectively, FDR's plan to fight the Depression was known as the New Deal, and it was a system of regulations, financial reforms, and government programs.

Part of the initial New Deal involved cutting government salaries and veterans' pensions to help balance the federal budget. FDR was a Democrat, but actions like these were fiscally conservative. However, the New Deal also included liberal measures like creating welfare and works programs to help struggling citizens. These had to be funded—and that funding resulted in deficits in the federal budget. One such program was the food stamp program, which was designed to help poor people provide food for their families. It is still

Two men in Chicago declare their eagerness to work in 1934, at the height of the Great Depression.

in use today. While the program was helpful for feeding the hungry in the 1930s and 1940s, in the twenty-first century, some fiscal conservatives have suggested that the program should be ended, believing that such assistance programs don't help end the problems of hunger and instead encourage people to remain on welfare programs.

FDR, widely regarded as a liberal, was fiscally conservative in some ways and fiscally liberal in others. While his terms in office did see the end of the Great Depression, the upturn in the economy cannot solely be credited to his economic policies. They did help the US economy begin to improve, but the outbreak of World War II also helped spur economic recovery. That's because many new jobs were created to support the war effort.

Another large recession in the past century was the Great Recession that began in 2007–2008. Like the Great Depression, the Great Recession was a worldwide economic crisis, though it is generally thought to have originated from instability in the United States economy. The US real estate market began to collapse in 2007 and continued to fall until about 2009. Around the same time, there was an international banking crisis and a shortage of financial assets. People lost their homes, their jobs, or both, and even those who held on to their homes lost valuable equity that they had gained.

When the recession began, a conservative president, George W. Bush, was in office. However, in 2008, a liberal president, Barack Obama, was elected, and he subsequently took office in 2009. Some people point a finger at President Bush for leading the country into a recession and laud President Obama for leading the country out of it. Others claim that President Obama is to blame for the recession, since he was in office during much of it.

A recession or depression doesn't happen because one president is in power. Recessions and depressions are the result of numerous factors that combine to form an economic collapse. Fluctuations in the economy are common—nations go through periods of prosperity and periods of hardship. Conservatives and liberals typically have different strategies for trying to boost a struggling economy, but there is no consensus on which strategy is the most effective.

Deregulation and Privatization

One way that conservatives try to strengthen the economy is through deregulation. Under liberal administrations, the government may put in place numerous regulations that limit the actions of certain industries. Laws surrounding environmental protection provide an excellent example. Under the liberal Obama administration, many environmental regulations were put into place as the administration worked toward encouraging greener sources of energy in an effort to combat the effects of global warming.

When the conservative Trump administration came to power, it immediately set about stripping regulations it felt to be unnecessary and detrimental to the US economy. For example, in March 2017, President Trump signed an executive order to dismantle the Clean Power Plan. The goal of the plan was to reduce harmful carbon dioxide emissions, especially from coal-burning power plants, while increasing the use of cleaner and renewable energy sources. Trump hoped to scale back regulations so his administration could bring back jobs in coal mining, which Trump insisted would put many unemployed coal miners back to work. Deregulation such as this is also a way to make government "smaller"—an effort common among conservative administrations.

Many conservatives are also in favor of privatization, which is when an industry becomes privately run by businesses or individuals rather than publicly run by the government. Conservatives argue that public control of industries leads to bigger government and unnecessarily increases government spending. They also insist that the government doesn't operate such programs as efficiently as private companies would.

Health care is a good example of an industry that can either be publicly run or privatized. In countries with socialized health care, such as Canada, the United Kingdom, and Sweden, the government generally runs the health-

At a 2009 rally in New York City, protesters insist that the American health-care system is in need of reform.

care industry. In the United States, the health care industry is something of a hybrid. Some people receive health-care coverage through their employer in a privatized system, but others receive health care through publicly funded services such as Medicare. During the Trump administration, there have been ongoing battles about whether to move the US further toward privatized health care. Liberals tend to favor the availability of publicly run health-care systems, whereas conservatives generally agree with the Trump administration that health care should be privatized.

In the mid-twentieth century, many industries were publicly run by the government. Beginning with the Reagan administration in the 1980s, there came a shift to privatization. Industries that could be run in the private sector were shifted that way, which decreased the number of necessary government regulations and, according to those in favor of privatization, reduced taxes, reduced the size of government, and helped the existing government run more efficiently.

Free Trade

Conservatives support free trade, which is a system in which there are no restrictions on imports and exports. Prices for goods and services are set by the demand in the global marketplace, rather than by government intervention or monopolies.

Free trade is widely thought to support healthy economic growth because it is driven by supply and demand—a common economic principle that suggests that the value of an item is determined by how much demand there is for it in the marketplace. Supply and demand has long been used in free markets to determine pricing.

However, opponents of free trade point out that it can lead to unemployment in the US job market. If consumers can readily obtain goods or services from overseas at a lower price than they can in the United States, it is likely that they will choose to do so, thereby putting US employees and business owners out of work. For example, a number of large companies outsource their customer-service or manufacturing jobs to other nations where people work for lower wages, costing jobs for Americans who might work in those areas.

One of the Trump administration's goals, according to its campaign, was to bring jobs back to the United States by redoing trade agreements that made it appealing for business owners to outsource jobs or import goods. Naturally, for Americans who may have been out of work, this idea can be appealing. However, the tariffs imposed on trade in an effort to quell outsourcing go against free-trade ideals and so do not align with most conservative ideologies.

SEAL OF THE PRESIDENT OF THE UNITED STATES

★ Chapter 4

Conservatism and Culture Today

Socially speaking, conservatives tend to value the traditions and institutions that are—or that they consider to be—foundations of the country. For example, social conservatives in the United States generally value the rights spelled out in the Constitution, the overall religious beliefs that were in place when the country was built, and social values from years past. Major changes to social values and traditions are often more widely embraced by liberals than by conservatives.

Reagan and the Establishment of Modern Conservatism

Conservatism in general (and social conservatism more specifically) has been a major ideology for generations, but under the Reagan administration, conservatism shifted into what it largely looks like today. Interestingly, Ronald Reagan was a liberal as a younger man, but in the post–World War II years, his beliefs changed, and he helped shaped the face of modern-day conservatism.

Opposite: Ronald Reagan, pictured here speaking in the White House rose garden, is considered by many to be the father of modern conservatism.

When Reagan took office, there were two major groups that made up the conservatives. There was the so-called Old Right, which was made up of people who greatly valued the original traditions and beliefs that were upheld when the United States was formed. The Old Right conservatives tended to be deeply religious and were often Catholic.

The second group was the neoconservatives, who mainly came from farther left on the political spectrum. The liberal left at that time had a fairly large base of radicals who favored major social changes that some less left-wing liberals weren't comfortable with. Some of those skeptical liberals eventually embraced conservative views, though they tended not to be as far right as the Old Right. For example, the Old Right wanted to dismantle welfare programs, whereas neoconservatives wanted to keep welfare programs but revise them to make them more efficient.

As more neoconservatives joined the Republican Party, the influence of the Old Right decreased. Around that same time, a third group of conservatives began to form: the New Right. In terms of belief systems, the New Right fell in the middle between the Old Right and the neoconservatives. They weren't as far right in their beliefs as the Old Right, but they definitely held more traditional values than neoconservatives, whom they viewed as relatively moderate in their beliefs.

The Christian Right, who believed strongly in Christian foundations informing American society, laws, and beliefs, saw allies in the New Right, and the two groups worked together to try to bring more religious influence into American society. This was just a few years after the *Roe v. Wade* case that made abortion legal nationwide—a Supreme Court decision that conservatives generally didn't agree with. As a result, conservatives worked to try to preserve traditions

Senator Ted Cruz of Texas is pictured during a "pro-family" rally in South Carolina in 2015. Cruz is a Christian conservative.

and laws wherever possible, and to keep religion as a basis for law and tradition.

Libertarians entered the scene around this time too. Libertarians staunchly believe in small government and argue that citizens should have a great deal of autonomy and be responsible for their own lives. In the eyes of libertarians, the less government intervention, the better.

Ronald Reagan managed to bring together all the diverse branches of conservatism that existed when he took office. Reagan's mission as president was to rebuild the nation's economy and to defeat communism, which was a looming power largely led by the Soviet Union, or USSR. In attempting to carry out his mission, Reagan drew ideas from all branches of conservatism and put them to use. This gained him the support of a wide range of conservatives.

President Ronald Reagan (*second from left*) leads a meeting on the deficit.

Where controversial issues were concerned, such as abortion and the backlash against *Roe v. Wade*, Reagan generally stood aside and returned focus to his mission to rebuild the economy and defeat communism. It was a shrewd and unifying political move. If Reagan had tackled abortion, for example, he would have gained much support from the Christian Right and probably the Old Right, but perhaps lost the support of some neoconservatives, who made up a large part of the Republican Party.

Reagan's efforts to rebuild the economy were similarly appealing to all sectors of conservatism. He wanted to both scale back government and make what government *did* exist run more efficiently. His plan didn't include a large-scale dismantling of government programs, which would have likely turned neoconservatives against him; it simply involved making calculated cuts and then working to ensure the remaining government ran more effectively.

Reagan had a generally likable personality and the political sense to make all sectors of the conservatives buy into his policies. The same can't necessarily be said of later conservative politicians.

The Evolution of Twenty-First-Century Conservatism

Reagan was the president who really shaped the face of conservatism in the late twentieth century. When his two terms in office were up, he was followed by another conservative president, George H. W. Bush. However, Bush, who had previously been Reagan's vice president, only served one term of his own. The nation entered an economic recession while he was in office, and the conservatives who had voted for him in 1988 were disappointed when he raised taxes in 1990 despite proclaiming in his 1988 campaign that he would *not* raise taxes. So, in the 1992 presidential campaign, Bush lost significant support that he'd had in 1988, and he was defeated by Democrat Bill Clinton.

For the next eight years, a Democratic president was in office. Clinton was not terribly far left, though. He was considered a moderate Democrat whose policies were fairly centrist.

In 2001, conservatives returned to the White House when George W. Bush (son of George H. W. Bush) took office. The younger Bush referred to his political philosophy as "compassionate conservatism"–his policies were conservative, but they were driven by a desire to improve the welfare of people and society, rather than being driven by a desire to stick to tradition.

Senator John McCain, a Political Maverick

It's relatively unusual for a politician to go against their party, but Senator John McCain from Arizona always *did* consider himself a maverick. McCain had a long and distinguished career in Congress, after being a prisoner of war in Vietnam for more than five years. A member of the Republican Party, McCain ran for president against Barack Obama in 2008 but was defeated. He continued to serve in the Senate until his death in August 2018.

Before losing a battle with brain cancer, McCain took a surprising stand that will likely land him a place in the history books. One of Donald Trump's missions as president was to

Senator John McCain speaks on the Senate floor on July 25, 2017, a few days before casting the deciding vote against a repeal of the Affordable Care Act.

dismantle the Affordable Care Act (ACA), which was passed by President Obama. The ACA was controversial because it provided an opportunity for all Americans to receive health care, but it was not necessarily the most efficient program—it was widely agreed that the ACA needed some fixes. Trump's solution was to completely repeal the ACA, which liberals heatedly disagreed with. Many conservatives disagreed too, feeling that modifications were needed to the ACA but that repealing it with no other plan in place would cause more problems than it would solve. However, most Republicans in Congress went along with the Trump administration and voted in July 2017 to repeal the ACA, despite their concerns.

John McCain was one of three standouts in the Republican Party who tipped the vote so that the repeal ultimately failed. The other two—Senators Susan Collins and Lisa Murkowski—had been firm all along that they would vote against the repeal. Collins's and Murkowski's votes alone would have made the repeal vote a tie, which would have been broken by Vice President Mike Pence, a conservative Republican who undoubtedly would have voted to pass the repeal. When McCain cast his vote, he killed the repeal—a surprise move that shocked the Senate and delighted Senate Democrats.

President George W. Bush, who held office from 2001 to 2009, espoused "compassionate conservatism." His policies were conservative, but they were also motivated by a desire to improve the welfare of people and society.

Under both George W. Bush administrations, conservatism as an ideology or movement didn't see a major shift like it had when Reagan was president. When Bush's second term ended, the liberal citizens in the United States, and some left-leaning conservatives, wanted a big change and elected Democrat Barack Obama to be president. This was a groundbreaking moment: President Obama was the first African American president of the United States.

President Obama promised a lot of changes that appealed to liberals. He did not keep all of his promises, but under the Obama administration, certain social changes took place. Perhaps the biggest shift came with the *Obergefell v. Hodges* decision by the Supreme Court, which guaranteed same-sex couples the right to marry in all fifty states.

While the president has no decision-making power in the Supreme Court, the president does nominate Supreme Court justices, which are then approved by the Senate. Democrat Bill Clinton appointed two liberal justices to the Supreme Court during his presidency: Stephen Breyer and Ruth Bader Ginsburg. President Obama appointed two liberal justices during his time in office as well: Sonia Sotomayor and Elena Kagan. All four of these justices have strengthened the liberal ideology on the court, which in turn informed the decision made on *Obergefell v. Hodges*.

Social changes, such as marriage equality, do not necessarily reflect the preference of all Americans. There are a fair number of citizens who would prefer that marriage still be limited to being between a man and a woman, and who would prefer that other liberal policies not have shaped American society. In 2016, the presidency shifted back to the conservatives when President Donald Trump won over Democratic nominee Hillary Rodham Clinton.

President Donald Trump, pictured in 2018, has been a controversial president who at times has lacked the support of conservatives as well as liberals.

President Donald Trump is a largely conservative president, though some of his positions range across the political spectrum. However, President Trump's supporters lean toward very conservative. He gained much support from the religious right, from the working class—which has broadly grown in its support of the Republican Party—and from people who want to see the United States go back to a far more conservative social philosophy.

This is not to say that all conservatives support President Trump, however. He is a highly controversial president who has upset people across the political spectrum and around the world. Liberals and even moderate conservatives often express a lack of support for him.

Trump does propose policies and legislation that are favored by conservatives. If he ends up enacting what he proposes, it remains to be seen whether he will regain the support of the conservatives who do not care for his presidency.

The Future of Conservatism

The United States is always shifting back and forth between liberal and conservative ideologies, and that swing will probably continue. At the moment, the future of conservatism is unclear because there seem to be larger ideological divisions between the dominant political parties. The next conservative to come to power may need to have the personality and the political shrewdness of Ronald Reagan to reconnect supporters of the conservative ideology who have found themselves very divided in recent years.

Chronology

1929 The stock market crash marks the beginning of the Great Depression.

1932 Liberal Democrat Franklin Delano Roosevelt is elected president of the United States.

1973 TheSupreme Court decision in *Roe v. Wade* legalizes abortion nationwide, a victory for liberals but a blow to conservatives.

1980 Ronald Reagan is elected president of the United States. Republicans dominate the Senate for the first time in nearly three decades.

1988 As Reagan's term comes to an end, conservative Republican George H. W. Bush is elected president of the United States.

1992 The presidency turns to the Democrats with the election of Bill Clinton.

2000 Another conservative enters the White House when George W. Bush is elected president.

2007 The United States enters the Great Recession, triggered by the housing crash.

2008 Moderate liberal Barack Obama is elected president of the United States.

2009 Liberal Sonia Sotomayor is confirmed to the Supreme Court.

2010 Liberal Elena Kagan is confirmed to the Supreme Court.

2014 Republicans win control of both houses of Congress.

2016 Conservative Republican Donald J. Trump is elected president of the United States.

2017 Conservative Neil Gorsuch is confirmed to the Supreme Court.

2018 John McCain, a Republican senator known for breaking with his party, dies. Conservative Brett Kavanaugh is confirmed to the Supreme Court.

Glossary

authoritarian conservatism A far-right ideology centered around nationalism and with a strong influence from religion, tradition, and culture.

autonomy Independence and freedom from external influence or control.

capitalism Economic system in which private business owners control a country's trade and industry.

Christian Right A right-wing ideology that espouses socially conservative policies influenced by religion. Also known as religious conservatism.

cultural conservatism A right-wing ideology that values the preservation of a nation's heritage or cultures.

depression A prolonged, severe economic decline.

deregulation The removal of restrictions and rules in a particular industry.

equity The money value of a property.

executive branch The branch of US government that includes the president and his or her cabinet.

fiscal conservatism An ideology and economic philosophy that emphasizes lowering government debt and spending, and keeping taxes low.

free market An economic model in which competition between private businesses determines prices.

ideology A system of ideals that form the basis of economic or political theory.

judicial branch The branch of US government that includes the Supreme Court and lower federal courts.

legislative branch The branch of US government that includes the lawmaking bodies of Congress: the House of Representatives and the Senate.

legislator A lawmaker.

liberal conservatism An ideology that embraces both conservative policies and liberal views, including minimal interference from the federal government but a strong state government.

libertarian A person who believes in free will and every citizen exercising their civil liberties to make their own decisions.

libertarian conservative A right-wing ideology that embraces small government, economic freedom, and general civil liberty.

magazine A chamber that holds multiple bullet cartridges that can be fed automatically into a gun.

Medicaid A federally run health insurance system that is available to people who require financial assistance or are disabled.

moderate A person who has views that fall in the middle of the political spectrum, rather than being far left-wing (liberal) or far right-wing (conservative).

monarchy A system of government led by a sovereign head of state, such as a king, queen, or emperor.

monopoly A company that has exclusive control over a particular good or service.

national debt The amount of money that a country's government has borrowed.

neoconservative A modified form of traditional conservatism that still has an emphasis on free-market capitalism.

Old Right An informal name used to describe conservatives who belonged to the group before neoconservatives emerged.

originalist A person who believes that the United States Constitution should be interpreted in the way that the drafters of the Constitution intended it when written.

precedent An earlier legal case whose decision must be followed in later similar cases.

privatization The transfer of a business, industry, or service from public to private ownership and control.

recession A time of economic decline in which the gross domestic product (GDP) falls for at least two successive quarters, and trade and industry are reduced.

repeal To take back or cancel a law.

rhetoric Language that is intended to persuade and may lack complete sincerity.

social conservatism An ideology that believes traditional values and long-established institutions are the bedrock of society.

supply-side economics An economic plan that attempts to increase output and employment by reducing regulations and taxes.

USSR Abbreviation for the Union of Soviet Socialist Republics, a federation of communist countries in eastern Europe and northern Asia that was created after World War I and dissolved in 1991.

welfare Financial support programs designed to help people who are in need.

Further Information

Books

Berlatsky, Noah. *The Republican Party*. Opposing Viewpoints. Farmington Hills, Michigan: Greenhaven Press, 2015.

Fleischer, Jeff. *Votes of Confidence: A Young Person's Guide to American Elections*. San Francisco: Zest Books, 2018.

Jacobs, Thomas A., and Natalie Jacobs. *Every Vote Matters: The Power of Your Voice, from Student Elections to the Supreme Court*. Minneapolis: Free Spirit Publishing, 2016.

McPherson, Stephanie. *Political Parties: From Nominations to Victory Celebrations*. Minneapolis: Lerner Publications, 2015.

Ziff, John. *The Modern Republican Party*. American Politics Today. El Dorado, Kansas: Eldorado Ink, 2016.

Websites

The Primaries Project

https://www.brookings.edu/project/the-primaries-project

This site, run by the Brookings Institution, is a great place to learn about what's going on in primary elections and in the two major political parties in the United States.

Supreme Court of the United States

https://www.supremecourt.gov

The official website for the Supreme Court contains a wealth of information about court opinions and filings, as well as oral arguments and case documents.

White House

https://www.whitehouse.gov

The White House website is always changing, depending on which party is in power, but under the Trump administration, it is a good place to look at the policies and issues currently of concern to many conservatives.

Videos

Conservatism: History, Ideology, and Influence

https://study.com/academy/lesson/conservatism-history-ideology-and-influence.html
This educational video offers a short history of conservatism and an overview of the ideology. Hypothetical examples illustrate the fundamental tenets of conservatism.

Is Trumpism the New Conservatism?

https://www.youtube.com/watch?v=pk4z0yo1u5M
A video from the *Atlantic* magazine analyzes whether President Donald Trump's version of conservatism signals what the future may hold for the ideology.

What Is Conservatism?

https://www.politico.com/video/2018/02/25/what-is-conservatism-065133
This video from *Politico* includes interviews with attendees from a large conservative conference to show how people defined conservatism in 2018.

Bibliography

"Are You Conservative or Liberal?" WordPress at LPS. Accessed October 16, 2018. http://wp.lps.org/tnettle/files/2013/12/Liberal-vs-Conservative.pdf.

Caldwell, Leigh Ann. "Obamacare Repeal Fails: Three GOP Senators Rebel in 49-51 Vote." NBC News, July 28, 2017. https://www.nbcnews.com/politics/congress/senate-gop-effort-repeal-obamacare-fails-n787311.

"Curriculum: National and State Standards." Education World. Accessed October 16, 2018. https://www.educationworld.com/standards.

Goodman, John B., and Gary W. Loveman. "Does Privatization Serve the Public Interest?" *Harvard Business Review*, November–December 1991. https://hbr.org/1991/11/does-privatization-serve-the-public-interest.

Hayward, Steven F. *The Age of Reagan: The Conservative Counterrevolution: 1980–1989*. New York: Crown Forum, 2009.

Heywood, Andrew. *Political Ideologies: An Introduction*. London, UK: Palgrave Macmillan, 2017.

"Historical Debt Outstanding – Annual." TreasuryDirect. Accessed October 16, 2018. https://www.treasurydirect.gov/govt/reports/pd/histdebt/histdebt.htm.

"New York State Regents Exams." New York State Library. Last updated October 8, 2018. http://www.nysl.nysed.gov/regentsexams.htm.

Political Ideology Among the Unaffiliated by Race/Ethnicity." Pew Research Center, 2014. http://www.pewforum.org/religious-landscape-study/compare/political-ideology/by/racial-and-ethnic-composition/among/religious-tradition/unaffiliated-religious-nones.

"Presidential Executive Order on Promoting Energy Independence and Economic Growth." White House, March 28, 2017. https://www.whitehouse.gov/presidential-actions/presidential-executive-order-promoting-energy-independence-economic-growth.

Saad, Lydia. "Conservative Lead in U.S. Ideology Is Down to Single Digits." Gallup, January 11, 2018. https://news.gallup.com/poll/225074/conservative-lead-ideology-down-single-digits.aspx.

Schneider, Gregory L. *The Conservative Century: From Reaction to Revolution*. New York: Rowman & Littlefield Publishers, Inc. 2009.

Seaton, James. *Cultural Conservatism, Political Liberalism: From Criticism to Cultural Studies*. Ann Arbor, Michigan: University of Michigan Press, 1996.

Van Til, L. John. "Ronald Reagan and the Changing Face of Conservatism." The Center for Vision & Values, July 7, 2004. http://www.visionandvalues.org/2004/07/ronald-reagan-and-the-changing-face-of-conservatism.

Zeppos, Nicholas W., and Philip A. Wallach. "Tracking Deregulation in the Trump Era." Brookings, December 5, 2017. https://www.brookings.edu/blog/fixgov/2017/12/05/tracking-deregulation-in-the-trump-era.

Index

Page numbers in **boldface** refer to images.

About the Author

Cathleen Small is the author of more than fifty nonfiction books for children and teens. Small is also a legislative advocate and the cochair of the California Down Syndrome Advocacy Coalition. Small believes in nonpartisan advocacy and has allies on both sides of the political spectrum.